WELCOME TO MY JOURNEY

This book is dedicated to my dear friend, Elizabeth Kranz,
because without you, I never would have found Sunny.
This book is also dedicated to anyone who has ever donated their time
or money, fostered or have adopted a rescue animal.
Thank you for everything you have done to help better those animals' lives!

#AdoptDontShop

5

Looking at the pup, who was just a poor stray.
The volunteers found him a place he could stay.

11

12

13

19

 The End

THANK YOU TO OUR CONTRIBUTORS

Daffodil Flores
Ben Riccardi
Sandra Tordella
Tom Farnan
Meg Kelly
Quinn Anderson
Cindy Nguyen
Richard Estes
Leah Wingeart
Rich Colbert
Danny Gomez
Jessica Rose
Anthony Nguyen
Sebastian Schubl
Kaitlyn Logan
Brian Wilbor
Maria Habermann

Rustyn Lee
Kayte Foley
Susan Michael
Pj Perez
David Lecroix
Susan Brisson
Paul MacKinnon
Brianne Spellane
Julio Morales
Ted Jeffcoat
Jim Garvey
Leticia & Ross
Krentzman
Eva Kenny
Jared Anderson
Nicholas Binger
Sonia Fernandes

Patrick Kenny
Adam Kaphan
Meaghan Tordella
Aaron Rossini
Hugh Geiger
Cristina Lebron
Jeremy Feldman
Jennifer Polmateer
Richard Horsch
Florence Yang
Janice Le-Nguyen
David Shahrestani
Scott Woods
Jayne Hadley
Philip Loomis

VOLUNTEER AND ADOPTION INFORMATION

If you live in the greater NYC area and are looking to donate and/or rescue an animal, look no further than Social Tees Animal Rescue. They coordinate missions in Los Angeles, and various parts of Missouri and Tennessee (which is where Sunny came from). They welcome volunteers in transporting the animals to and from the airport, fostering, and donations, so that they may continue their rescue efforts.

www.socialteesnyc.org

VOLUNTEER AND ADOPTION INFORMATION

If you live in the greater Las Vegas area, the Nevada SPCA is an outstanding organization to look into. They are currently undergoing a massive upgrade to their main facility, which will allow them to rescue even more animals than they already do! They are also looking for people to volunteer their time at adoption events, become foster parents and for anyone who can provide monetary donations to their cause.

www.nevadaspca.org

Rescuing one animal may not change the world, but for that one animal, their world is forever changed —be that change.